An Anchor for My Soul Devotions

SOUL ANCHORING DEVOTIONS FOR THE MULTIFACETED, MULTI-TASKED WOMAN

Sister - Mother – Daughter – Wife - Minister – Professional – Mentor - Woman

By Lenita Reeves

PurposeHouse Publishing

Lenita Reeves is the founder of PurposeHouse Publishing, PurposeHouse Biblical Counseling, and Real Life. Real Change. Unashamed. She is a member of the RAINN speakers' bureau and an international conference speaker. She is the author of *Fervent Fire: Understanding the Pattern of the Priesthood for Prevailing Prayer* and other books. For more information, visit www.lenitareeves.org. For a full list of all her books, visit www.amazon.com/author/lenitareeves.

PurposeHouse Publishing, Columbia, Maryland

Copyright © 2020 Lenita Reeves. All rights reserved.
ISBN: 978-1-7329549-2-2

Cover design by PurposeHouse Publishing, all rights reserved.

No part of this publication may be reproduced or distributed in any form or by any means, or stored in a database or retrieval system, without the prior written permission of the publisher. Email requests for permission to ministeringpurpose@gmail.com.

Unless otherwise indicated, all scriptural quotations are from the King James Version of the Bible, which is in the public domain.

Scripture from Amplified Bible (AMP, Copyright © 1987 by the Lockman Foundation. (www.Lockman.org)

Scripture from the Contemporary English Version (CEV), Copyright © 1995 by American Bible Society

Scripture from the Living Bible (TLB), Copyright © 1971 by Tyndale House Foundation, Used by permission of Tyndale House Publishers Inc., Carol Stream, Illinois 60188. All rights reserved.

Scripture from the Message Bible (MSG), Copyright © 1993, 1994, 1995, 1996, 2000, 2001, 2002 by Eugene H. Peterson. All rights reserved.

Scripture from the New International Version (NIV), Copyright © 1973, 1978, 1984 by Biblica

Scripture from New King James Version (NKJV), Copyright © 1982 by Thomas Nelson, Inc., All rights reserved.

Scripture from the New Life Version (NLV), Copyright © 1969 by Christian Literature International

Scripture from the New Living Translation (NLT), Copyright © 1996, 2004 by Tyndale Charitable Trust

Scripture from the Wycliffe Bible (WYC), Copyright © 2001 by Terence P. Noble

Dedication

I dedicate this book to women all over the world. Women who are mothers, sisters, wives, daughters, friends, and ministers of the gospel—all at the same time. You juggle so much. You do multiple things and prioritize multiple people every day. May God's Word, grace, and peace keep you anchored.

Contents

Introduction 11

1: Lord, Why Do I Have to Do Everything Myself? 13

2: Information Overload 17

3: Vulnerable Once Again 21

4: Your Validation 25

5: Are you there, God? It's me <your name>. 29

6: Look in the Mirror 33

7: Ruler of a City: Modeling Self-Discipline for Our Daughters 37

8: A Family Affair 41

9: Destined 45

10: You're not Superwoman 49

11: A Great Cloud of Witnesses 53

12: Don't Faint 59

13: Daughter of Sarah 63

14: A Mother's Authority 67

15: Are You Wearing Your Coat Well? 71

16: Daughter = Full-time disciple 75

17: Clear the Way 79

18: Enemy Number One: Comparison 83

19: Don't Give Up: Dominate 87

20: You Can Break the Line 91

21: A Pre-Midlife Crisis Moment 95

Bonus: The Multifaceted Model: The Proverbs 31 Woman 99

Real Life. Real Change. Unashamed. 107

Acknowledgements

I want to say a big thank you to my mother. Thank you for every obstacle you overcame, and every moment of love and encouragement you were able to share with us even in the midst of the struggle. God bless you.

 # Introduction

Today's Christian woman is faced with a dilemma, and its name is "multi-." While trying to serve the Lord, multiplicities of responsibility vie for her attention. She wrestles daily to handle it all and simultaneously understand her multifaceted nature. But unfortunately, helping others often prevents the healing of issues within her soul.

An Anchor for My Soul Devotions addresses these issues, facilitates healing, and anchors Christian women who are dizzy and discombobulated from the whirlwind of multiple responsibilities, talents, and roles. Before a ship sets sail, it must be anchored and refueled. This twenty-one-day devotional is the multitasked, multifaceted woman's necessary daily dose of anchoring and refueling.

Devotions for the Multifaceted, Multi-tasked Woman

1: Lord, Why Do I Have to Do Everything Myself?

The multiple pressures of life can cause you to feel as if you are the only one going through what you are going through. Having lived the life of a single mother, I understand the pressure and anxiety that can occur when the smallest frustration arises at just the wrong moment. For example, after a long day at the office, the mental anguish of the unjust work environment plays through your mind. At the same time, your child cries, the bill collector calls, your clothes get stained from cooking—and to top it all off—the food burns while you're on the phone! It's enough to make anyone throw up their hands, break down in tears and cry, "Lord, why do I have to do everything myself?"

In those moments, you can find solace and peace in a God who declares, "I will never leave you nor forsake you." When you reach those breaking points, you must overcome every emotion within yourself. Remember that "His yoke is easy, and his burden is light," even when it feels like a ton of bricks! It's okay to break down in tears as long as when you are down there, you manage to whisper one word, help.

His strength is made perfect in your weakness. Be encouraged by the fact that God is ever with you. He will never leave you, nor will he forsake you. Even when you feel alone (yes, it is our feelings that get the best of us in those situations), the truth that he is always there doesn't change. He loves you and cares for you. Not only are you not alone, but also, he is *your* helper. You don't have to do it alone. What you and I *can* do is ask for assistance, depending on our helper to come through.

Scripture Focus

For he hath said, I will never leave thee, nor forsake thee. So that we may boldly say...The Lord is my helper, and I will not fear what man shall do unto me. (Hebrews 13:5a-6 KJV)

An Anchor for My Soul

Prayer Focus

Lord, in times of frustration, help me to master my emotions and focus on the truth of your presence with me and your willingness to help me.
(Write your own prayer below.)

Reflect

1. How do you usually respond to frustration? Be honest and don't overestimate yourself. What's your usual, initial response?

2. Does your usual, initial response reflect the presence of a loving helper?

3. When was the last time you rested in his presence?

4. Read Psalm 91:1-3 NLT. Is it possible to rest during what should be a frustrating experience?

Devotions for the Multifaceted, Multi-tasked Woman

Devotions for the Multifaceted, Multi-tasked Woman

2: Information Overload

Do you ever feel like you have so much information, but you are paralyzed and don't know what to do? There are many days when I return from work, mentally exhausted. Though my body could go on for hours, my mind sends up a white flag and screams, "Sit down for a second: I need a break!"

It is oh so familiar. I get home from work, and my son asks me the simplest question. Still, answering seems to exhaust every faculty within me. I have processed so much information and made so many decisions during the day. The amount of information we now process daily is phenomenal. I won't even try to quote the latest statistic because it is always changing—increasing that is. Nonetheless, the woman who must consider herself, and her job, finances, husband, children, and ministry, has an overwhelming amount of information to process.

Today, we have access to information on top of information. But, in the valley of all that information, wisdom is the necessary factor. You need the understanding to take actions that lead to success for you, your family, and everything and everyone under your care.

You can have what seems like all the right information and still have no peace about what you are supposed to do with it. The Bible says, "For wisdom is better than rubies; and all the things that may be desired are not to be compared to it" (Proverbs 8:11 KJV). Having lots of information is no substitute for the peace of knowing its proper application. The information presented may indicate that it's time to move forward, but the fear of God would advise you to wait until God says go. In whatever decisions you are facing, and will face today, ask God for his wisdom to know what to do and how to do it. The Bible declares that our Father is always willing to share with us his timeless wisdom. Don't get stuck by information overload. Ask God for wisdom.

Scripture Focus

If any man lack wisdom let him ask of God who giveth liberally and upbraideth not. (James 1:5 KJV)

Wisdom is defined as: the ability to discern or judge what is true, right, or lasting; insight ability to discern inner qualities and relationships; insight; good sense; judgment.

An Anchor for My Soul

When I'm mentally fatigued and faced with critical decisions, give me wisdom to know what to do and when to do it.
(Write your own prayer below.)

Reflect

1. What situation(s) are you facing that require God's wisdom to achieve the best outcome for you or someone under your care?

2. If you move out of tiredness or fatigue without God's wisdom, what are some potential effects? What will waiting for God's wisdom prevent?

An Anchor for My Soul

Notes

3: Vulnerable Once Again

As leaders in ministry, work, and home, people often look to us for support in hard times; times when everyone else is falling apart and the expectation of us is to be the calming voice of encouragement and reason. As nurturer-leaders, we are everyone's source of refuge and support when things fall apart. Our husbands seek quiet solace in our arms when the pressures of life mount. Our children run to us for protection. Young women look to us for guidance and counsel in their times of trouble. But who is there for us, the mother-minister-wife, when we need encouragement? It is easy to give, give, give, and never stop to receive a renewing touch of God's love.

Even more dangerous is the woman leader who, because of hurt and fear of rejection, is afraid to stop her activity. She gains validation from her much doing. The enemy uses it to her detriment. She runs ragged with all the activity until she loses focus on the beauty of intimate fellowship with the Father. Amazingly, it often takes more strength to be still and not do anything than to be active.

If the Lord is calling you into a season of stillness (lesser activity), don't be afraid to say no to requests for your time and talents. God sometimes uses that to remind us that even when we are not busy "doing," he still loves us. When we strive to earn validation and love, we've overlooked the fact that we didn't earn salvation through works but by grace.

If you're striving, cease from your striving and rest in the love and presence of God. Draw nigh to God, and he will draw nigh to you. Be vulnerable. Ask God to fill you with his love and adjust your motivations for serving and doing. Let go of doing, and trust God to pour out his love on you. Be vulnerable once again.

Scripture Focus

But Martha was cumbered about much serving, and came to him, and said, Lord, dost thou not care that my sister hath left me to serve alone? bid her therefore that she help me. And Jesus answered and said unto her, Martha, Martha, thou art careful and troubled about many things: But one thing is needful: and Mary hath chosen that good part, which shall not be taken away from her. (Luke 10:40-42 KJV)

Prayer Focus

Father, help me to cease from my much serving and seek the good part which is your presence. Let my service come as an overflow of the love I experience daily in your presence so that I can serve without frustration, comparison, or striving. (Write your own prayer below.)

Reflect

1. Are you involved in any activity that you should eliminate or delegate to someone else?

2. Is there any physical person in your life that encourages and brings balance to your life?

3. Are you enjoying intimate fellowship with the Father on a regular basis?

Devotions for the Multifaceted, Multi-tasked Woman

4: Your Validation

Images of the present-day culture paint a picture that we often accept as the standard for our lives. We measure how we feel about ourselves against society's expectations of us, and it is reflected in the statements we make. Words such as, "By now I should have been married, by now I should have my own house, by now my husband and I should have children, by now I should be a size six." But may I kindly ask, who told you 'by now' was the right time? By making such statements, we perpetuate the mindset of the society [the world] and place undue pressure on ourselves to achieve a standard that didn't originate with God. Also, we exempt ourselves from enjoying our present state. We are preoccupied with the condition that society has told us we should be in, instead of enjoying where we are currently positioned. It is a vicious cycle of discontentment.

Thanks be to God! You can break the cycle. Breaking it involves primarily the renewing of your mind and an acceptance of what the Word of God has to say about you. Your validation doesn't come from reaching "society's benchmarks" but from pleasing God. Godliness with contentment is great gain. He is your validation.

Scripture Focus

Perverse disputings of men of corrupt minds, and destitute of the truth, supposing that gain is godliness: from such withdraw thyself. But godliness with contentment is great gain. For we brought nothing into this world, and it is certain we can carry nothing out. (1 Timothy 6:5 KJV)

Prayer Focus

Father, help me to realize that my validation does not come from the accumulation of things or worldly stature. Please help me to be grateful for where

you have brought me thus far, and to enjoy the moments you've given me now instead of worrying about tomorrow.
(Write your own prayer below.)

---

1. Reflect on your current goals and desires. Is each connected to God's plan for your life, or to the standards of society?

2. Is there any discontentment in your life and why?

3. What can you do to focus on God's goodness in your life and thank him for what he's already done?

An Anchor for My Soul

Notes

Devotions for the Multifaceted, Multi-tasked Woman

5: Are you there, God? It's me <your name>.

Have you ever wondered if God was with you? At times, the bitter disappointments of life are enough to drive a wedge between our God and us. Sometimes, we get knocked back by the enemy's fiery darts and the unwieldy circumstances of life. We get so caught up in our daily activity that we neglect the quality time needed to keep our relationship with God (or any relationship for that matter) vital and vibrant. We've all been there. Disappointment sets in, and it's hard to pray. Then, a cycle of guilt begins, and we feel even farther away from God.

Breaking the cycle involves a simple decision and recognition that God is waiting for us. The scripture says, "Draw nigh to God, and he will draw nigh to you." Even though we feel that we've slipped so far away, all he wants is the faintest gesture towards him. With the subtlest yet sincerest cry for help, he's right at our side.

Guilt and condemnation are not from God. If you have not prayed as you should, ask God to forgive you; then draw nigh by setting your affection on him. When you open your arms, he will, in turn, open his, giving you a welcoming, reassuring embrace. He is always there. Draw nigh.

Scripture Focus

Draw nigh to God, and he will draw nigh to you. Cleanse your hands, ye sinners; and purify your hearts, ye double minded. (James 4:8 KJV)

Prayer Focus

Father, it has been a while since I spent quality time with you, but I give you my heart right now and draw close to you. As your word has promised, I know you will draw close to me.
(Write your own prayer at the top of the next page)

1. Are you conscience of God's presence with you throughout the day?

2. What new steps can you take to draw closer to God?

Devotions for the Multifaceted, Multi-tasked Woman

An Anchor for My Soul

Devotions for the Multifaceted, Multi-tasked Woman

6: Look in the Mirror

The steam from the hot shower filled the entire bathroom like the vapors from a smoky fire. Tammy lavished the warm mist that swept across her face. She was so pleased that she had managed to clean the house and get the laundry done—on the same day! To top it all off, little Julia lay fast asleep; Tammy finally had time alone to take a peaceful shower. Her face was glowing with a grin from ear to ear. Suddenly, it happened. Tammy caught a glance of herself in the mirror while drying off—her smile disappeared.

Looking at ourselves in the mirror is one of the most evaluative things we do as human beings. The amazing thing is that usually, we don't say a spoken word. Yet we manage to communicate so loudly to our conscience through a silent look, sigh, or physical adjustment (sucking in) of the stomach. In that silent, evaluative moment, we loudly communicate the mantra and state of our self-esteem, as Tammy did when her smile disappeared.

I'll admit that moment is sometimes depressing. We notice last week's potatoes that went right to the thighs, and we feel a moment of defeat. However, in those silent moments, we must speak [to ourselves] what the word of God has to say about us and maintain a proper perspective. I believe the proper perspective is a realization that God never commanded us to be "sexy." God commanded us to be modest and healthy. It is our society that places upon us the demand to compete with re-touched, false images of busty, scantily dressed models. You and I are not commanded to follow such a mandate.

If you need to lose weight for your heath's sake, do it, but don't place undue pressure on yourself to be something God never called you to be. I encourage you to speak God's truth about yourself when you look in the mirror. Let the presence of God shine through you today.

Beloved, I wish above all things that thou mayest prosper and be in health, even as thy soul prospereth. (3 John 1:2 KJV)
For thou hast possessed my reins; thou hast covered me in my mother's womb. I will praise thee; for I am fearfully and wonderfully made: marvelous are thy works; and that my soul knoweth right well. My substance was not hid from thee, when I was made in secret, and curiously wrought in the lowest parts of the earth. (Psalm 139:13-15 KJV)

Prayer Focus

Father, when I look in the mirror, please help me to speak what you say about me. Help me to focus on caring for my body, which is your temple, so that it is healthy, rather than focusing on a worldly, unrealistic image and expectation. (Write your own prayer below.)

Reflect

1. When you see or walk by a beautiful woman, do you begin to feel inferior or uneasy about the way you look? Is your reaction in line with the word of God? Do you try to hide your feelings by taking on a prideful or haughty disposition? If so, why?

2. Do you lead a healthy lifestyle, which includes fasting, exercise, and sensible eating? What steps are you taking to maintain your health?

3. Would you say that your opinion of yourself is in line with God's word? How can the word of God help your self-esteem?

Devotions for the Multifaceted, Multi-tasked Woman

7: Ruler of a City: Modeling Self-Discipline for Our Daughters

The times demand multiplicity, multitasking, and multi-talents. Women work outside the home, participate in ministry (whether full-time or part-time), encourage their husbands, raise their children, and put dinner on the table by 7 pm. Of all the roles, the profoundness of having a full-time disciple, a daughter, is sometimes the most overwhelming responsibility to fulfill.

I often wonder what my daughter thinks when she watches me. What goes through her mind when she sees me praying or reading the Bible? When she sees me worship, what goes through her mind? I may never know the intricate details, but I do know that she will imitate what she sees me do. I am creating a life-culture with every action I take, after which she will model her life and her own family.

With all the interactions she will observe me engage in, I realize that the most crucial observation she will make is how I interact with myself. She will observe my self-discipline or lack thereof, and she will model her standards for herself based on what she sees. It is easy to be the strong manager on the job or the model Christian in the church building, but our children see who we are when we are at home, and no one is looking. With our multiple talents, we may be able to conquer the world, but what's more important is that we conquer ourselves. Let's ask God for grace to take time today, and every day, to model self-discipline for our children.

Scripture Focus

He that is slow to anger is better than the mighty; and he that ruleth his spirit than he that taketh a city. (Proverbs 16:32 KJV)

He that hath no rule over his own spirit is like a city that is broken down, and without walls. (Proverbs 25:28 KJV)

Prayer Focus

Heavenly Father, today I pray for my daughter. I pray that your counsel, mind, and original intent for her life will come into manifestation, that she will grow in grace, and become the woman you've called her to be. Give me the grace to model the kind of self-discipline she will need.
(Write your own prayer below.)

Reflect

1. If your daughter eats what you eat, will she be healthy?

2. If your daughter prays the way you pray, will she have a strong prayer life?

3. In what new ways can you model self-discipline for your daughter?

Devotions for the Multifaceted, Multi-tasked Woman

An Anchor for My Soul

Notes

8: A Family Affair

My mother made sure we went to church on Sundays. It was expected. It was a given. If we went out on Saturday with friends, we knew we would have to come home and prepare for church the next day. After God drew me to himself and gave me a personal experience with him that went beyond "just going to church," I realized that my childhood church had some things lacking. But I appreciate the fact that my mother exposed us to God and gave us what she knew of God at that time. Once I began to know God personally, God took me away from my family and put me in a place that he could get my attention. He told Abraham to get out of his father's country, and James and John left their father and his hired servants on the boat and straightway followed Jesus. God sometimes pulls us away from our family to get our attention, groom us, and grow us. But there comes a time when he sends us back to share the beauty of the relationship with him that he took us away to experience. To this day, I am baffled at how hard it can be to witness to my family members. They are so familiar to me, yet they are sometimes strangers. The me they knew is not the real me that God has quickened. I am a puzzle to them, and they are a prayer burden to me. I guess that you can relate to this. Perhaps you are still believing God for an unsaved family member? Hold on to the word of God and keep praying. Find the courage to love them, spend time with them, and share the gospel with them. God may pull us away for a season, but he intends to prepare us to go back. John 1:41 amazes me. It says that after experiencing Christ, Andrew first went and told his brother. Is there a brother or sister that you need to tell that you've encountered the Messiah? Find the courage today. Share a word with them and let God water the seed that you plant. Andrew first experienced the Messiah, but, Peter, his brother, was used mightily to take the gospel to the Jews. You may be the forerunner for your family. Still, your sibling, mother, or father may hold the keys to an entire nation or generation. Don't hold back; you may be holding the destiny of nations.

Scripture Focus

He saith unto them, Come and see. They came and saw where he dwelt, and abode with him that day: for it was about the tenth hour. ⁴⁰One of the two which heard John speak, and followed him, was Andrew, Simon Peter's brother. ⁴¹He first findeth his own brother Simon, and saith unto him, We have found the Messias, which is, being interpreted, the Christ. ⁴²And he brought him to Jesus. And when Jesus beheld him, he said, Thou art Simon the son of Jona: thou shalt be called Cephas, which is by interpretation, A stone. (John 1:39-42 KJV)

Prayer Focus

Lord, let your goodness extend to my family members. Bring my unsaved loved ones to a place of repentance, and let the scales that blind them from receiving the gospel fall from their eyes.
(Write your own prayer below.)

Reflect

1. What unsaved family member do you need to re-commit to prayer?

2. How can you demonstrate the love of God to your unsaved family members?

Devotions for the Multifaceted, Multi-tasked Woman

9: Destined

des·ti·ny (noun): *1. The inevitable or necessary fate to which a particular person or thing is destined; one's lot. 2. A predetermined course of events considered as something beyond human power or control. (www.dictionary.com)*

One day, I overheard my husband singing a song in the living room. He was sitting at the piano, gently stroking the keys, and singing the words:

*"I have a destiny I know I shall fulfill. I have a destiny in a city on a hill.
I have a destiny. It's not an empty wish.
For I know, I was born for such a time as this."*

As he sang, something inside me immediately connected with the song. But it was more than a connection; it was a longing—a heavy desire. Destiny unfulfilled cried out, and the hope of fulfilling it swelled up in my soul. It felt like a lump in the back of my throat trying to expand. Holding back tears, I whispered, "God let me fulfill your will for my life and use the gifts and talents you've given me the way you want me to. Please let me be everything you've ordained me to be."

At that moment, I knew it was all within my reach. It was possible, but it would take discipline and a drive that I needed to cultivate daily. I knew that I would have to maintain my responsibilities as a mother and a wife while pushing hard into the apostolic ministry God had ordained for me. I knew it would cost me sleep, discipline, and sweat. But, at that moment, I had, in fact, counted the cost. In my spirit, I looked forward, never to look back. It didn't matter that I had failed. It didn't matter that life wasn't perfect. It didn't matter that I didn't have a title. It just didn't matter. All that mattered was in my spirit, I knew the time had come, and finally, my mind and soul had come into agreement with that knowing. I encourage you to look ahead. Be everything God ordained you to be. In every area of your life, live, and produce to your full potential. The God inside you is big enough to do it. He's waiting for you to live as if it is so.

Scripture Focus

In him we were also chosen, having been predestined according to the plan of him who works out everything in conformity with the purpose of his will, in order that we, who were the first to hope in Christ, might be for the praise of his glory. (Ephesians 1:11-12 NIV)

Prayer Focus

Lord, let your divine purpose for my life manifest. Let all hindrances to the full counsel of God for my life be destroyed.
(Write your own prayer below.)

Reflect

1. Identify one thing you know you are called to accomplish in the earth. What steps are you taking towards completing it?

2. Is there any aspect of your destiny that you have neglected because of procrastination and why?

3. Have you spent time fasting and praying about your destiny? Could it be time to do so?

An Anchor for My Soul

10: You're not Superwoman

"Women have more efficient access to both sides of their brain and therefore greater use of their right brain. Women can focus on more than one problem at one time and frequently prefer to solve problems through multiple activities at a time."
– Michael G. Conner, Psy.D., Clinical and Medical Psychologist

Even before the release of the popular book, *Men are from Mars, Women are From Venus*, it had long been accepted that women have an innate capacity to multitask and process information with both sides of their brain. Many women are climbing the corporate ladder or assuming more responsibility in other areas. Also, the fast pace of today's society and the many demands of everyday life intensify the need to multitask. Many gifted and talented women can keep pace with these increasing demands. More women are completing higher education, buying homes, and establishing themselves without men. Yes, we are taking over the boardroom and bringing home larger paychecks than our male counterparts.

But with all this success, the danger is becoming overly confident in our own abilities—in the flesh. Have you ever taken on too much and found that you were not doing any of it in excellence? Have you ever been overconfident in your own skills and found that your success is actually the product of God's grace and not your own ability? In all our doing, we must remember that it is not by might and not by power, but by the Spirit of God. Even though it seems you can handle it all: you're not superwoman. There's no doubt that you are gifted, but you must maintain humility. Remember, your gift will make room for you, but you must know how to walk in humility to stay in the room.

He that refuseth instruction despiseth his own soul: but he that heareth reproof getteth understanding. 33 The fear of the LORD is the instruction of wisdom; and before honour is humility. (Proverbs 15:32-33 KJV)

An Anchor for My Soul

Prayer Focus

Lord, thank you for my gifts and abilities. I recognize you as the source and know that they came from you. Help me to be a woman of humility.
(Write your own prayer below.)

Reflect

1. Are there any areas of your life that you are not walking in humility?

2. In what new ways can you honour God and give him the glory for your gifts and abilities?

An Anchor for My Soul

11: A Great Cloud of Witnesses

On January 1, 2005, Shirley Chisholm died; on October 24, 2005, Rosa Parks died; and on January 30, 2006, Coretta Scott King died. Consider the great women who died over one year. Specifically, consider the greatness of their contributions to African American history and society.

In 1968, Shirley Anita St. Hill Chisholm became the first African American woman elected to Congress. On January 23, 1972, she became the first African American candidate for President of the United States. Chisholm won 162 delegates. Before Hilary Clinton, she was the closest any woman has ever come to winning the nomination for president by a major party.

On December 1, 1955, Rosa Parks became famous for refusing to obey bus driver James Blake's order that she give up her seat. This act of civil disobedience started the Montgomery Bus Boycott, one of the largest movements against racial segregation. Also, this launched Martin Luther King, Jr., who was involved with the boycott, to a position of awe among his people. She has had a lasting legacy worldwide.

Coretta Scott King was the wife of the assassinated civil rights activist, Martin Luther King, Jr., and a noted community leader. Coretta King is a recipient of the Congressional Gold Medal.

What will the world be like without them? Who will fill their shoes? These women achieved much. They faced racism and limitations head-on. When you and I consider our small trials, I can safely assume that these women endured them and much more. Yet, they conquered heights that men and women of other races and ethnicities could not.

The Bible speaks of a great cloud of witnesses. I wonder what Shirley, Coretta, and Rosa would have to say of you and me as they look down? Clearly, they embraced the multi-. They were women, wives, mothers, and societal leaders. What excuses can be mustered in the face of women of such caliber?

Rosa Parks took a single decision that changed her destiny forever. Consider her words on what went through her mind as she came to a decision:

> "I did not want to be mistreated; I did not want to be deprived of a seat that I had paid for. It was just time... there was an opportunity for me to take a stand to express the way I felt about being treated in that manner. I had not planned to get arrested. I had plenty to do without having to end up in jail. But when I had to face that decision, I didn't hesitate to do so because I felt that we had endured that too long. The more we gave in, the more we complied with that kind of treatment, the more oppressive it became."

Shirley Caesar, who thank God is still with us, recalled her early days on an episode of the "60 Minutes" television show. She stated that by age thirteen, she was performing. Caesar toured and remembered white men beating up the pastor and the pastor's wife; she ran, and they didn't catch her. She wrote her own request to do a solo, and because of that, she was asked to sing with the Caravans. Caesar stated that she never sang secular or pop because she heard the Lord say, "I've ordained you to preach the gospel." That single decision (a decision not to compromise) has blessed countless thousands.

What decision do you have to take? You and I indeed have a great cloud of witnesses and the testimony of great women who have gone before us. I am challenged to consider them and ask why we still allow excuses to hinder our dreams and callings. If they achieved, we can too.

Scripture Focus

> *Wherefore seeing we also are compassed about with so great a cloud of witnesses, let us lay aside every weight, and the sin which doth so easily beset us, and let us run with patience the race that is set before us, Looking unto Jesus the author and finisher of our faith; who for the joy that was set before him endured the cross, despising the shame, and is set down at the right hand of the throne of God. For consider him that endured such contradiction of sinners against himself, lest ye be wearied and faint in your minds. Ye have not yet resisted unto blood, striving against sin. (Hebrews 12:1-4 KJV)*

Devotions for the Multifaceted, Multi-tasked Woman

Prayer Focus

Lord, help me to lay aside every weight that keeps me from running the race, the path, which you have ordained for my life. Help me to make the decisions that will propel me into my destiny. Thank you for the example of great women who have gone before me. Their lives testify to the fact that it is possible to handle multiple responsibilities gracefully and accomplish great things with my life.
(Write your own prayer below.)

Reflect

1. God's call for us often seems overwhelming. How does the example of Shirley Chisholm, Rosa Parks, Shirley Caesar, or Coretta King affect your thoughts about your own destiny and calling?

2. The cloud of witnesses that has gone before us lived for a cause greater than themselves. Have you identified a cause for which you live? Is that cause worth embracing the "multi"?

Devotions for the Multifaceted, Multi-tasked Woman

12: Don't Faint

It is often said that life is more like a marathon than a sprint. With each lap of life, there are new challenges, seasons, relationships, opportunities, and, hopefully, new triumphs. In the world of athletics, specifically in the arena of track and field, sprinters train differently than distance runners. The emphasis in one event is power, while in the other it is persistence.

Coreperformance.com lists "running out of fuel" as one of the top ten marathon training mistakes. When your body runs low on energy, it breaks down fuel stores. Then your speed suffers, the run feels harder, your mechanics break down, and performance dips. And it's not just about your pre-race meal. "If you're not eating enough carbohydrates in general, then it won't make a difference what you eat right before your training," says Carlson of Coreperformance.com.

If life is more like a marathon, then consider that running out of fuel is symbolic of running out of prayer when it comes to our walk with God. In the same way that a runner cannot rely on the pre-race meal for all their necessary nutrients, believers cannot wait until times of crisis to pray. Persistence is of greater importance than isolated bursts of power.

"Nothing in the world can take the place of persistence. Talent will not; nothing is more common than unsuccessful men with talent. Genius will not; unrewarded genius is almost a proverb. Education will not; the world is full of educated derelicts. Persistence and determination alone are omnipotent." - Calvin Coolidge

"If the word quit is part of your vocabulary, then the word finish is likely not." - B.G. Jett

Scripture Focus

And he spake a parable unto them to this end, that men ought always to pray, and not to faint; ²Saying, There was in a city a judge, which feared not God, neither regarded man: ³And there was a widow in that city; and she came unto him, saying, Avenge me of mine adversary. ⁴And he would not for a while: but afterward he said within himself, Though I fear not God, nor regard man; ⁵Yet because this widow troubleth me, I will avenge her, lest by her continual coming she weary me. ⁶And the Lord said, Hear what the unjust judge saith. ⁷And shall not God avenge his own elect, which cry day and night unto him, though he bear long with them? ⁸I tell you that he will avenge them speedily. Nevertheless when the Son of man cometh, shall he find faith on the earth? (Luke 18:1-8 KJV)

Prayer Focus

Father, give me the grace to be persistent in prayer.
(Write your own prayer below.)

Reflect

1. Do you have a consistent, appointed prayer time with God?

2. In what new ways can you refuel your prayer life and intimacy with God?

An Anchor for My Soul

13: Daughter of Sarah

The greatness of Father Abraham is undeniable. He is called the 'father of faith,' and we know that "Abraham believed God, and it was imputed unto him for righteousness: and he was called the Friend of God" (James 2:23). Given that, I have always wondered how Sarah felt when her husband, the man who was supposed to be her covering and the great 'father of faith,' lied and said she was his sister. At first consideration, I thought, "How can a sell-out be the friend of God?" And what is even more amazing is Sarah's response to him [Abraham]. In the account of Abraham telling the king that Sarah was his sister (Genesis 20), the Bible never records Sarah yelling, screaming, or giving Abraham a piece of her mind. Even while she was in the king's house, there was no record of resistance, but God himself spoke to the king before any intimacy could occur. Think about it. She was about to have her own "night with the king"—by no fault of her own. The Bible does not record her sticking her lips in the air and giving Abraham attitude, but rather, the Bible says this of Sarah: *"Even as Sara obeyed Abraham, calling him lord: whose daughters ye are, as long as ye do well, and are not afraid with any amazement"* (1 Peter 3:6 KJV).

When I consider this, I am challenged to humble myself and change my reactions to my husband's weaknesses. God is indeed the God who qualifies the called rather than calling the qualified. In our consideration of Sarah, we can see that God's strength is made perfect in weakness. Consider this; Sarah laughed within herself at the promise that she would bear a child. Even worse, she lied in God's presence and said she did not laugh (Genesis 18). But despite her laughing and lying, she is one of the few women recorded in the Hebrews chapter eleven hall of faith. Isn't that just like God? Where did this woman who laughed at the promise of God find the strength to become a rock in the face of her husband's fear? If you and I will simply believe God, we will also see the promises of God manifested in our lives. First Peter 3:6 encourages us not to be afraid with amazement. Do not be afraid when the weaknesses of those you count on shock you or take you by surprise. Continue to honor them and love them. Believe God to see a change in them, despite human weakness, and you will be a daughter of Sarah.

Scripture Focus

Even as Sara obeyed Abraham, calling him lord: whose daughters ye are, as long as ye do well, and are not afraid with any amazement. (1 Peter 3:6 KJV)

Prayer Focus

Father, help me to honor those in authority in my life, even when it seems they don't deserve honor.
(Write your own prayer below.)

Reflect

1. In what new ways can you show honor and respect for your husband? If you are single, consider this question considering your future marriage (if you want to get married).

2. Christ loves us when we are not lovely. How can you show love to your husband in times when he seems unlovely?

Devotions for the Multifaceted, Multi-tasked Woman

An Anchor for My Soul

14: A Mother's Authority

As Christians, we hear stories about the horrible behavior of pastors' kids. They [the pastors' kids] cause their parents such pain and embarrassment, and we wonder how "the apple could fall so far from the tree." While we are musing about the situations of these leaders, it never occurs to us that it could be our child that loses their mind momentarily and ends up in juvenile court, pregnant, or worse. But when it hits us that our children have two worlds and two personalities, one for their church world and one for their school world (which we know nothing about), our insides collapse, and disappointment overtakes us. At that moment, we have two choices. We can give up and let the devil have our children, or we can fight and stand on God's word.

Children from the best homes and the 'most Christian' homes (if there is such a thing) can end up in the worst situations. For those parents who love their children, and passionately want to see them serve God, such events can shake the very foundations of their faith. They ask the question, "God, I'm serving you. How could this happen to *my* children?" The reality is the devil doesn't play fair, and if you are truly serving God, he [the devil] wants your children even more.

Today, if you are confronted with a rebellious child or a child who is not living up to their full potential in God or school—don't take it lying down. Stand on the word of God. Reclaim your children and your authority in their lives as a parent. You run the show; you set the standards; you dictate the rules! Stand on the word, which says:

- Foolishness is bound in the heart of a child, but the rod of correction shall drive it far from him. (Proverbs 22:15 KJV)
- Withhold not correction from the child: for if thou beatest him with the rod, he shall not die. (Proverbs 23:13 KJV)
- Train up a child in the way he should go: and when he is old, he will not depart from it. (Proverbs 22:6 KJV)

Many of us have become so programmed by the world system that we don't want to correct our children. Children need correction, and they need it from their parents. Take a stand today, and in love and care, correct your children and set the record straight. It is better for you to do it than for the police to have to. Rise up and be courageous.

Scripture Focus

Withhold not correction from the child: for if thou beatest him with the rod, he shall not die. (Proverbs 23:13 KJV)

Prayer Focus

Father, give me the courage to correct my children. Give me the strength to not give up or grow weary. I choose to fight for my children.
(Write your own prayer below.)

Reflect

1. Remember, your children are worth the fight. They have a calling and a purpose. What has God shown you about your child's (children's) assignment on earth?

15: Are You Wearing Your Coat Well?

This world is full of people's opinions. People will give you a piece of their mind, whether solicited or unsolicited. Even in the church, hidden agendas based on people's opinions prevail, and people don't treat others as they should. If you don't know who you are, someone else will impose an identity on you. So the question I want to ask you today is, "Are you wearing your coat well?"

Yes, each of us has a coat of favor that the Father himself has woven for us; a garment in the Spirit that is perfectly suited for us—tailored to the tee. But if you allow fear, intimidation, rejection, or unbelief to rule over you, you will never slip your arms into that coat. You will be wearing polyester when God has destined you for linen and silk.

People may look at your life and wonder how you got where you are—let them look. They may say you don't deserve to be blessed the way you are. You know the line, "How did *she* end up with him?" How did she get a husband, children, a ministry, and a high-paying career? I came to tell you that you are entitled to all of that and more. Stop telling yourself it's beyond your reach, and drive out the voice of doubt and unbelief. Where were they (the naysayers) when you were at home on Friday nights praying instead of compromising your purity? Where were they when you sowed your seed in tears in obedience to God? I don't know, and you don't know, but the bottom line is, who cares what naysayers say?

As our friend Joseph found out, real favor invokes jealousy, but you and I can rise above it and love despite it. Girlfriend, put your coat on and strut it. Accessorize it with gold, and don't forget your perfume. You can't help it if God favored you. Even when Joseph's brothers taunted him, the Bible says his father brooded over the whole business (Genesis 37:11 The Message Bible). God is holding your dream to his heart, and he's ready to make it a reality if you will only step out in faith and believe him. Walk in your favor.

Scripture Focus

For thou art the glory of their strength: and in thy favour our horn shall be exalted. (Psalm 89:17 KJV)

Prayer Focus

Lord, let your favor be activated in my life. Let me walk in the confidence of your unmerited goodness. I now know that your favor goes beyond my ability to be perfect. Still, it will propel me into my destiny even as the favor that Esther found in the site of the king promoted her. It positioned her to enter her destiny. Let your goodness work for me like the favor that Joseph found with the king's cupbearer. As Potiphar positioned him to fulfill his destiny, let me be placed. Cover my life with your favor, in Jesus's name.
(Write your own prayer below.)

Reflect

1. Consider a time when God showed you unmerited goodness or opened a door for you that you did not deserve? How did it impact your confidence?

2. Think about how the favor of God might be working in your life right now.

16: Daughter = Full-time disciple

And the two disciples heard him speak, and they followed Jesus. Then Jesus turned, and saw them following, and saith unto them, What seek ye? They said unto him, Rabbi, (which is to say, being interpreted, Master,) where dwellest thou? He saith unto them, Come and see. They came and saw where he dwelt, and abode with him that day: for it was about the tenth hour. (John 1:37-39 KJV)

When the disciples heard Jesus speak, they followed him. They were moved in their hearts by what they heard. They wanted to be up close and personal with the man that had captured their beings with words of life. To follow him fully, they knew they had to spend more time with him; so, they dwelt with him and saw the place where he lived.

People want to spend time with those they admire or that add something of value to their lives. In the case of the disciples, they saw in Jesus their destiny and followed without reservation. An attitude of "purposeful following" is a thing of power. When we as individuals follow another without reservation or consideration of reputation, we position ourselves to be tremendously vulnerable, and, at the same time, hugely blessed.

I see this same attitude in my daughter. She opens her heart to me completely, and she believes that her father and I can do anything. She, in many ways, is like a blank canvas ready for me to apply paint skillfully. She is my full-time disciple. She not only sees the place where I dwell (as the disciples did with Jesus), but her life is shaped and defined by it.

As mothers, it warms our hearts when we see the love that our children have for us. The challenge comes when we are pulled by other responsibilities and lack the energy we need to properly disciple (discipline) our children. I just want to encourage you today, that even though you may be tired from work, ministry, or other things, take time to discipline your children. Put their care at the priority it should be. It is not always easy, but you and I must paint the canvas and do our part to ensure that it becomes a masterpiece.

"Our children are our full-time disciples, a canvas whose beauty we are responsible to craft." – Lenita Reeves

Scripture Focus

My son, despise not the chastening of the LORD; neither be weary of his correction: For whom the LORD loveth he correcteth; even as a father the son in whom he delighteth. (Proverbs 3:11-12 KJV)

He that spareth his rod hateth his son: but he that loveth him chasteneth him betimes. (Proverbs 13:24 KJV)

Chasten thy son while there is hope, and let not thy soul spare for his crying. (Proverbs 19:18 KJV)

Correct thy son and he shall give thee rest; yea, he shall give delight unto thy soul. (Proverbs 29:17 KJV)

Prayer Focus

Lord, I receive new strength and focus to raise my child(ren) and bring them up in the way you have determined they should go. Help me to correct them in love and see them give me rest.
(Write your own prayer below.)

Reflect

1. What skills will your child need to be a successful adult?

2. What can you do to prepare him or her to handle multiple responsibilities?

3. Would you say that you have accepted your role to disciple your children)?

An Anchor for My Soul

Devotions for the Multifaceted, Multi-tasked Woman

17: Clear the Way

Steven Covey's rocks and sand illustration for prioritizing and time management has become extremely popular. We understand the concept; put the big rocks in the bowl first, and you can pour the small sand in around it. But put the small sand in first, and the big rocks won't fit in the bowl. He uses this practical illustration to drive home the point that we need to focus on the major life priorities first. It is such a simple principle. Yet we nod our heads in agreement, then walk away and do the exact opposite.

Martha, the sister of Mary, suffered from the same amnesia, which I call "Martha Syndrome." She was distracted by sand when the chief cornerstone was in her midst. We think of prioritizing when we sit down to plan or to organize our day at work. However, many of us catch "Martha Syndrome" when it comes to other things like our relationships and personal development.

Have you put more energy into doing the work of the church than knowing the God of the church? Have you put more effort into reminding your husband of the things on the to-do list that he has not completed than reminding him of how much you love and respect him? Have you put more energy into driving your kids to activities than spending time with them or praying with them? Even good things can be distractions when they cause us to neglect needful things. Jesus warned Martha to put the clutter aside and put the big rocks in first.

"And Jesus answered and said unto her, Martha, Martha, thou art careful and troubled about many things: But one thing is needful: and Mary hath chosen that good part, which shall not be taken away from her" (Luke 10:41-42 KJV).

Notice that she was so distracted that he had to call her name twice to get her attention! De-cluttering involves choosing what is needful. Even on popular, home decorating and improvement television shows, such as *Mission Organization*, participants must choose what to put in the *keep pile* and what to put in the *junk pile*.

When Jesus told Martha to choose what was needful, it wasn't that he didn't want to eat or receive her hospitality. He was telling her to seize the moment for what it was offering her. Many times, God directs us to put focus and effort into certain areas, and we resist because we don't feel we can do so and keep the laundry clean every week. Yes, the laundry is important, but no one is going to die if they have to do their own laundry for a week. Don't resist God's pull into a greater depth of focus because you are troubled about many things. Seize the opportunity and the grace that God releases to you at that moment. It may just be the season for you to learn of God at a greater level, or it may be the season of preparation God ordained for you to be promoted. Choose the good part. De-clutter your life and clear the way for your individual move of God. Don't be so distracted with tasks that you don't take time to love the people closest to you.

Scripture Focus

Now it came to pass, as they went, that he entered into a certain village: and a certain woman named Martha received him into her house. 39 And she had a sister called Mary, which also sat at Jesus' feet, and heard his word. 40 But Martha was cumbered about much serving, and came to him, and said, Lord, dost thou not care that my sister hath left me to serve alone? bid her therefore that she help me. 41 And Jesus answered and said unto her, Martha, Martha, thou art careful and troubled about many things: 42 But one thing is needful: and Mary hath chosen that good part, which shall not be taken away from her. (Luke 10:38-42 KJV)

Prayer Focus

Lord, I thank you for the grace to remove distractions from my life. Help me to prioritize my time with you, and the things that are most important to you. Free me from Martha Syndrome. In Jesus's name, I pray.
(Write your own prayer below.)

Reflect

1. Is there anything you are fretting about or worried about that is fostering a "Martha Syndrome" in your life?

2. What are the "big rocks" you need to prioritize?

An Anchor for My Soul

Devotions for the Multifaceted, Multi-tasked Woman

18: Enemy Number One: Comparison

For we are His workmanship [His own master work, a work of art], created in Christ Jesus [reborn from above—spiritually transformed, renewed, ready to be used] for good works, which God prepared [for us] beforehand [taking paths which He set], so that we would walk in them [living the good life which He prearranged and made ready for us]. (Ephesians 2:10, Amplified Bible (AMP))

When you find a "One Size Fits All Garment" in the store, it's usually because the designer has deemed it big enough to fit almost all body types and sizes. Women come in all body types and sizes, and the role of a wife, mother, sister, entrepreneur, or friend is not "one size fits all." It's not cookie-cutter; meaning, there's not a single pattern for the role(s) you take on. Some women's primary profession is serving their husbands and children as stay-at-home moms. In contrast, others work in Corporate America. Yet, others serve in ministry, having the responsibility to help govern the affairs of the church.

Often, women are confronted with varied responsibilities and competing priorities. And because the "grass always seems greener on the other side," they often compare themselves to one another. Scripture warns against this, stating:

We do not dare to classify or compare ourselves with some who commend themselves. When they measure themselves by themselves and compare themselves with themselves, they are not wise. (2 Corinthians 10:12 NIV)

When God designed us, he didn't design "one size fits all" assignments. Instead of comparing yourself to other women, focus on finding out what God requires of you as an individual believer, endowed with gifts, and predestined for good works. In the end, we will all stand before God alone, giving account for the gifts that God placed in us—gifts that he endowed us with for a particular assignment during our time on earth. We are all God's workmanship created in Christ Jesus for good works that we should walk in them (Ephesians 2:10 KJV). Each woman brings something unique to the kingdom of God and the body of Christ. Discover who you are in him. Discover the cut of your cloth; because, when it comes to calling, there is no "one size fits all."

An Anchor for My Soul

Scripture Focus

Each one's work will be clearly shown [for what it is]; for the day [of judgment] will disclose it, because it is to be revealed with fire, and the fire will test the quality and character and worth of each person's work. (1 Corinthians 3:13, AMP)

Prayer Focus

Lord, help me to discover my gifts, passions, and assignment on earth so that I can stand boldly before you on the Day of Judgment and hear, "Well done." In Jesus's name, I pray. Amen.
(Write your own prayer below.)

Reflect

1. Review Ephesians 2:10 and consider what works God has assigned you to do in the earth? Have you started to do these works? If not, why? If so, how can you further your effectiveness in your assignment?

Devotions for the Multifaceted, Multi-tasked Woman

19: Don't Give Up: Dominate

And Adam gave names to all cattle, and to the fowl of the air, and to every beast of the field; but for Adam there was not found an help meet for him. (Genesis 2:20 KJV)

So God created man in His own image, in the image and likeness of God He created him; male and female He created them. 28 And God blessed them [granting them certain authority] and said to them, "Be fruitful, multiply, and fill the earth, and subjugate it [putting it under your power]; and rule over (dominate) the fish of the sea, the birds of the air, and every living thing that moves upon the earth." (Genesis 1:27-28, AMP)

According to the Creation27 journal, Adam named approximately 2,500 proto species of animals, birds, and livestock during creation. They estimate that it would have taken Adam three hours and forty-five minutes to name them all. That's assuming he was naming them at a rate of one animal every five seconds. After he named the animals, birds, and livestock, God put him in a deep sleep and formed Eve from his side. Amazingly, even though Adam had never seen another human being, as soon as he saw Eve, he exclaimed, "This is now bone of my bones and flesh of my flesh." Adam had been sleeping during the whole surgery and had never seen another human being, yet he knew Eve came out of him.

After naming 2,500 different types of animals, Adam understood that none of them was suitable to help him. They could not help him fulfill the one mandate he had been given—to take dominion (Genesis 1:27-28). God blessed them—male and female—and told them both to dominate. This means that the *dominion mandate* is a *co-dominionship mandate*. Meaning, you are the only animal designed, suited, and capable of joining your Adam—your husband (current or future)—in the dominion journey. And as a single woman, you have been blessed and empowered to take dominion.

Adam exclaimed, "This is now bone of my bones and flesh of my flesh," because he realized that Eve was made of the same "stuff" he was made of. She was not like the other 2,500 animals he had named. She was the only animal suitable for the "zoo of life" called "taking dominion." Likewise, you are perfectly suited for the dominion journey set before you. He placed that capacity in you at creation and blessed you to succeed in it. Rise up; don't give up. Take dominion!

Genesis 1:27-28 (listed above)

Prayer Focus

Lord, help me to dominate in life. You have already blessed me to take dominion. Thank you for empowering me for the assignment. In Jesus's name, I pray. Amen.
(Write your own prayer below.)

 Reflect

1. When God created mankind, he blessed male and female to take dominion. Are you living beneath your dominion mandate? How does God's blessing affect your confidence to move forward in dominion?

Devotions for the Multifaceted, Multi-tasked Woman

20: You Can Break the Line

And Jesus went with him; and much people followed him, and thronged him. [25] And a certain woman, which had an issue of blood twelve years, [26] And had suffered many things of many physicians, and had spent all that she had, and was nothing bettered, but rather grew worse, [27] When she had heard of Jesus, came in the press behind, and touched his garment. [28] For she said, If I may touch but his clothes, I shall be whole. [29] And straightway the fountain of her blood was dried up; and she felt in her body that she was healed of that plague. (Mark 5:24-29 KJV)

One of my least favorite activities is grocery shopping. Whenever possible, I try to order online. But sometimes, you just have to go into a physical store. When I do, I feel like I could be doing so many other things with the time spent walking the aisles. And the wait in line to check out is the worst! It really racks my nerves, especially when I've gotten more than fifteen items and can't use the express line. And now, with coronavirus, it's even worse. I hate being at the back of a checkout line.

The woman with the issue of blood found herself in a long, crowded line. More than my simple annoyance at the grocery store lines, this woman was facing seemingly insurmountable odds. She had been deemed unclean and was among a crowd of people who were stronger and faster. She was taking a risk to touch Jesus—against all the odds.

Life sometimes feels that way, like you are working against all the odds. But stop and ask yourself, how did she manage to break through the line? I believe it was more than sheer determination. After twelve years with no results, she must have been desperate. Her faith in other things (physicians and medicines) had waned, and now, she had found a new focus for her faith. Her faith was so focused and sure that Jesus felt virtue leave him.

Whatever you are facing, you can also overcome the odds. If your faith is focused, you can break the line. You can come from the back of the aisle and emerge triumphantly. Today, make sure you are reaching out to touch him, even the hem of his garment, and wholeness will be extended to you from his presence.

Scripture Focus

Mark 5:24-29 KJV (listed above)

Prayer Focus

Lord, let me my faith be genuinely focused on you. If I am still turning to other sources that cannot make me whole, help me to realize and admit it. Let my faith be active to touch you and receive virtue and strength from your presence. Whatever I have been carrying, I reach out to touch you and exchange it for your peace.
(Write your own prayer below.)

Reflect

1. Like the woman's twelve-year issue, is there any infirmity you have been carrying too long?

2. Have you focused your faith to touch Jesus concerning this issue?

Devotions for the Multifaceted, Multi-tasked Woman

An Anchor for My Soul

Notes

21: A Pre-Midlife Crisis Moment

The May 16, 2005, edition of Time Magazine asks the riveting question, "What does a female midlife crisis look like anyway?" During my lunch break at work one day, it occurred to me that I had had a *pre*-midlife crisis the night before. You see, the night before, I had driven to my mother's house after a 6:30pm–10:00pm class to pick up my daughter from her grandmother's third-floor condo. My sister, who was visiting my mother at the time, obliged my fatigue by bringing my daughter and her car seat down to the parking lot to meet me. When she [my sister] arrived downstairs, she was full of excitement, as if she had just won a new car or something. Having spent almost four hours in class, it was all I could do to brace myself for what was coming and muster the strength to concentrate on what she was about to say. "Here's my idea," she stated emphatically.

She went into detail about an idea that came to her. It was an idea that she felt was that one thing in life to which she could be genuinely devoted; it was something that fit her, and that would give her a sense of fulfillment. I listened to the eagerness in her voice, and it did more than wake me up from my tiredness. It caused me to evaluate what I was doing with my own dreams. Yes, at age thirty-two, I began to feel as if I had not accomplished much of what God really wanted me to do in life, and that time was running out of the hourglass.

Now, this may not qualify as a full-blown "mid-life crisis." But it was definitely a turning point. I must say, after that night, the insecurities of my past were not what came to mind when I begin to think about my God-given dreams. What came to mind was, "Okay, let's figure this out and get it done." You see, at age twenty, I had time to think about insecurities. Now, with the crisis in the Middle East, floods, volcanic eruptions, locusts in East Africa, coronavirus, and the impending sagging that is trying to take over my body, I figure I don't have time to worry about insecurities. Everything around me points to the return of Christ, and there's a voice yelling from the back of my head saying, "I'd better do what God really called me to do." If I don't, Jesus just might come back, and my chances to do something of impact will be over. Why waste another minute?" So-- perhaps my pre-midlife crisis was not a crisis but a turning point?

Any way you turn it, the time is now to throw insecurities out the door and reach for what you've always dreamed of doing. Yes, God takes us through the process and prepares us, but perhaps [and I say this with love and respect] you are the hold up to your dreams and not God? Take a step. Run to the finish line because everything around us indicates that we're in the final lap. You can still make a difference if you throw caution and insecurity to the wind. God is with you. Take the first step, then start running.

Scripture Focus

...but the people that do know their God shall be strong, and do exploits. (Daniel 11:32b KJV)

Prayer Focus

Father, if there are dreams that I have abandoned, revive them in my soul today. And give me the wisdom and strategies I need to execute them.
(Write your own prayer below.)

Reflect

1. Have you ever had a mid-life crisis or turning point? If so, what were your realizations?

2. When Joseph received dreams from God, his siblings didn't understand them, but his father held the matter close to his heart. Are there God-given dreams you have let go of?

Devotions for the Multifaceted, Multi-tasked Woman

Bonus: The Multifaceted Model: The Proverbs 31 Woman

After first reading Proverbs 31:10-31, my reaction was, "Was this woman actually real?" It seems she could do everything. In these twenty-one verses, we find several capabilities and qualities within a single woman. The following table lists them.

Proverbs 31:10-31 KJV (Verses)	Capabilities and Qualities
10 Who can find a virtuous woman? for her price is far above rubies.	The New International Version says, "who can find a woman of noble character?" Her *character* is noble.
11 The heart of her husband doth safely trust in her, so that he shall have no need of spoil.	She keeps her husband thoroughly satisfied. His heart wants for nothing else.
12 She will do him good and not evil all the days of her life.	Her love for him is not conditional. She is completely on his side.
13 She seeketh wool, and flax, and worketh willingly with her hands.	She had an eye out for the needs of her household.
14 She is like the merchants' ships; she bringeth her food from afar.	She could cook; not just one cuisine or style of food, but several. There was variety.
15 She riseth also while it is yet night, and giveth meat to her household, and a portion to her maidens.	She gets up early; while it is still dark outside.
16 She considereth a field, and buyeth it: with the fruit of her hands she planteth a vineyard.	She was a real estate investor. She had savings to develop land.
17 She girdeth her loins with strength, and strengtheneth her arms.	She was healthy (in shape) and strong.
18 She perceiveth that her merchandise is good: her candle goeth not out by night.	She didn't just work, she worked hard and long.
19 She layeth her hands to the spindle, and her hands hold the distaff.	She could make her own clothes and her apparel was fine.
20 She stretcheth out her hand to the poor; yea, she reacheth forth her hands to the needy.	Even though she had it going on, she was down to earth enough to extend her hand to the needy without looking down on them.
21 She is not afraid of the snow for her household: for all her household are clothed with scarlet.	She planned for the changing seasons of life.

22 She maketh herself coverings of tapestry; her clothing is silk and purple.	She had a personal sense of style.
23 Her husband is known in the gates, when he sitteth among the elders of the land.	Her husband wasn't a chicken head. He knew what he was about and where he was going.
24 She maketh fine linen, and selleth it; and delivereth girdles unto the merchant.	She was an entrepreneur.
25 Strength and honour are her clothing; and she shall rejoice in time to come.	She was honored and respected in the community. Laughter was her portion.
26 She openeth her mouth with wisdom; and in her tongue is the law of kindness.	She was a wise teacher. There was something everyone could learn from her.
27 She looketh well to the ways of her household, and eateth not the bread of idleness.	She managed her home. She was knowledgeable in areas of personal finance.
28 Her children arise up, and call her blessed; her husband also, and he praiseth her.	She had a great relationship with her children. Her husband loved and respected her, and he let her know it.
29 Many daughters have done virtuously, but thou excellest them all.	She walked in excellence.
30 Favour is deceitful, and beauty is vain: but a woman that feareth the LORD, she shall be praised.	She feared the Lord.
31 Give her of the fruit of her hands; and let her own works praise her in the gates.	Her own works testified of her character.

Yes, the virtuous woman seems to be a fable, a fictitious, immaterial description of an unattainable goal worth striving towards. Yet while we may not have mastered all her qualities and capabilities, we live aspects of this woman every day. Getting up early, working out, cooking, managing the finances, spending time with our children, and maintaining our personal sense of style are daily activities for most of us.

The nature of a woman's life has always been multifaceted. Modern times have amplified the situation by extending the "multi" nature outside the home. But even in biblical times, women's work was multifaceted. If there is an aspect of the multifaceted woman modeled in Proverbs 31 that you need to develop, know that it is possible. Take time to rise before day, and devise a plan. The virtuous woman is already inside of you because Christ is inside of you. Set a virtuous goal, plan for it, take action, and stick to it. You can be everything God has called you to be.

Devotions for the Multifaceted, Multi-tasked Woman

Scripture Focus

Proverbs 31:10-31 (listed above)

Prayer Focus

Lord, help me to handle the multiple responsibilities that come with being a virtuous woman. Give me a tangible action plan in the areas that I need to improve as well as the grace to implement the plan and see change.
(Write your own prayer below.)

Reflect

1. What qualities and capabilities of the Proverbs 31 woman do you currently possess?

2. What qualities and capabilities do you need to develop?

About the Author

Lenita Reeves is the senior pastor of Action Chapel Baltimore, a prophetic church under the covering of Archbishop Nicholas Duncan-Williams, who ordained her into ministry.

She is the author of several books including, <u>I Am: The Divine Purpose Manifesto</u>, <u>Fervent Fire, Breaking the Silence, The Spirit of Rejection, and I Am a Creative, Speaking Spirit.</u> And she is the founder of PurposeHouse Publishing, which helps others publish their books and meet their marketing needs.

As an abuse survivor and former teen mom, God has graced Lenita to be an outspoken overcomer, sharing her testimony freely and as a result, seeing captives set free all over the world. She is an international conference speaker and a member of the RAINN speaker's bureau. She has travelled the world to conduct apostolic missions and train leaders in London, Jamaica, Haiti, the Bahamas, Kenya, Uganda, and Ghana.

She began her service to the Lord in campus ministry. As Deputy Director of Campus Ministries United, she assisted in planting campus branches and the coordination of an annual conference aimed at bringing various campus ministries together in a night of prayer, praise, and relationship building. In the next phase of her ministry, God taught her the basics of pastoring while serving as a youth minister.

Some call her preacher and some call her teacher, but all agree that she is a prolific voice who speaks with transparency, highlighting her highs as well as her lows to show others that God can turn pain into a platform and use the foolish things of this world to confound the wise.

From senior class president to director in Corporate America to founder of a non-profit and pastor, leadership has been an evident mark of Pastor Lenita's life calling and passions. She has a Bachelor of Science in Industrial Engineering from Georgia Tech, a Master of Arts in Dance Education from the Ohio State University and an MBA from the University of Maryland, College Park. She is currently a doctoral candidate in Christian Counselling and attended Beulah Heights Bible College in Atlanta, Georgia, which was then under the leadership of Dr. Sam Chand.

Pastor Lenita was ordained in Action Chapel International in Ghana by Archbishop Nicholas Duncan-Williams and in Action Chapel North America by Bishop Kibby Otoo. She is married to Pastor Cephas Reeves and they have four children, Elijah, Cenita, Ethan, and Joshua.

For more information, visit www.lenitareeves.org.

Other Titles

I Am: The Divine Purpose Manifesto

I Am Predestined

I Am A Creative, Speaking Spirit

Fervent Fire: Understanding the Pattern of the Priesthood for Prevailing Intercessory Prayer

The Spirit of Rejection: Heal its wounds, Restore your Self-Esteem, and Move on to Promotion

Breaking the Silence: The Journey from Rape to Redemption

All available at Amazon.com!

Stay Connected

Discover the latest tools and encouragement for living on purpose! Visit www.lenitareeves.org and join our mailing list for the latest blog posts and continued news and previews of other upcoming books.

Visit us on social media

YouTube: Lenita Reeves

Web: www.lenitareeves.org

Facebook: http://www.facebook.com/pastorlenita

YouTube: http://www.youtube.com/pastorlenita

Instagram: http://www.instagram.com/pastorlenita

Devotions for the Multifaceted, Multi-tasked Woman

Real Life. Real Change. Unashamed.

Dear Precious One,

I pray that this book has been a blessing to you. There's something of urgency that I want to share with you. Please take the time to read this entire letter about a God-inspired project called, "<u>Real Life. Real Change. Unashamed.</u>" I'd like you to be a part of it. Please let me explain what this is and why it's essential at this time.

I'M ASKING FOR 7 MINUTES OF YOUR TIME. TWO MINUTES TO READ THIS BRIEF LETTER AND 5 TO HELP ME WIN A SOUL TO CHRIST. WILL YOU HELP WIN A SOUL?

Background

The day we live in is an era like none other. The signs of Jesus's imminent return are all around. As I write this, Kenya, Somalia, and Uganda have been battling swarms of locust in what is the worst outbreak that parts of East Africa have seen in seventy years. At least twenty-six tornadoes have been reported in Oklahoma, Texas, Louisiana, and Mississippi, with at least six people killed by the severe weather. And coronavirus—well—I don't have to say much about COVID-19. We all know the devastation and death it has caused. These events and more that I have not mentioned, are enough to make anybody stop and think.

Strategy

And that is what happened to me recently. As I read 1 Chronicles 12:32a KJV, which says, "And of the children of Issachar, which were men that had understanding of the times, to know what Israel ought to do," the Holy Spirit inspired me. He brought Matthew 24:14 NLT to my mind, "And the Good News about the Kingdom will be preached throughout the whole world, so that all nations will hear it; and then the end will come." Then, he reminded me that everyone was in crisis mode, but that's not the most important thing. The most important thing is the spreading of the gospel of the kingdom. And that is what Israel, the body of Christ, should be focused on right now. This is what Israel ought to do and be focused on right now.

So many churches are now turning to the digital space, it seems every preacher I know is now "going live." And you know what? I believe that's how it should be. However, I also believe that when we speak in that digital space, we must be intentional about articulating the gospel of the kingdom and inviting viewers to salvation. I believe the Lord whispered to me, "Flood the digital space with the message of salvation. That is the strategy for the Church at this time." We know that the world is functioning online right now—well, at least half of it. There are 7.7 billion people in the world, and according to Statistica.com, half of them are on the Internet. So why don't we capitalize on that to win souls?

Tactic/Implementation

What's my point, you ask? Winning souls is my point. I'm asking you to lay down titles, church competition, and any other barrier to help me flood the digital space with the message of salvation. And here's how:

1.) Use your cell phone's video camera and record your salvation testimony. Yes, it's that simple.
2.) Address the following four points in your video:
   a. Life Before Christ: What was your life like before salvation? Were you dealing with an issue?
   b. Your Encounter with Christ: How you came to a changed mind (repentance) and receiving Jesus/salvation?
   c. Life After Christ: What's the change? Meaning, how is your life different now?
   d. Invitation: Invite the viewer to receive Jesus through prayer and John 10:9-11 KJV.
3.) Send us the video, and we will use every means we have to share it in the digital space. You can email it, send a Google Drive link, or use wetransfer.com to the email address, ministeringpurpose@gmail.com.

Your video will help to accomplish the goal of flooding the digital space with the gospel and become what I believe will a repository and evangelism tool.

WOULD YOU TAKE 5 MINUTES TO HELP WIN A SOUL? IT WILL BE ADDED TO YOUR ACCOUNT IN HEAVEN.

Why is "*Real Life. Real Change. Unashamed.*" necessary?

It will help you and the entire body of Christ to win souls. How you ask? My first video is currently in the editing process. It features Michael, a former drug addict who has been set free and unashamedly volunteered to do the first video. He goes through the four steps. He explains what his drug-addicted life was like before Christ, how he met Christ, and how his life changed. Then, he leads the viewer in prayer and an invitation to receive Jesus. How much more effective might showing this video to a family member be than you trying over and over again to talk to them? Once more videos come in, you'll be able to search the "*Real Life. Real Change. Unashamed.*" video collection for the particular issue someone you want to lead to Christ is facing.

Let's act now!

Please don't hesitate; don't put this down and say I will do it later. It will only take you five minutes, so I beseech you to act now. You will have my deepest appreciation, but more importantly, God's. Thank you for taking the time to read this, and let's join to do whatever we can to spread the gospel. We don't know how much time we have left to do so.

Yours for a harvest of souls,

Lenita Reeves

The fruit of the righteous is a tree of life; and he that winneth souls is wise.
(Proverbs 11:30 KJV)

---

www.ingramcontent.com/pod-product-compliance
Lightning Source LLC
LaVergne TN
LVHW061216060426
835507LV00016B/1966